Life Cycles

John Stringer

Life Cycles 1

Seeds germinate. New plants shoot and grow. The new plant grows leaves and flowers. It does all this without being fed. Where does its energy come from?

The plant's secret is its leaves. The leaves of a green plant are its food factories.

Green leaves collect light energy. Most of the light energy comes from the Sun. The plant takes in water. It takes in a gas called **carbon dioxide** from the air.

The leaf uses these things to make food for the plant. The food stores energy. The leaf makes **oxygen** as well.

A green plant uses the food made in its leaves to live and grow. It uses the food to grow flowers and make seeds.

Animals and plants both need oxygen to use their food. A green plant uses some of the oxygen it makes. Animals cannot make oxygen for themselves. They need the oxygen from green plants to break down their food.

Animals produce carbon dioxide, which the green plants use. This picture shows that oxygen and carbon dioxide circulate between plants, animals and the air.

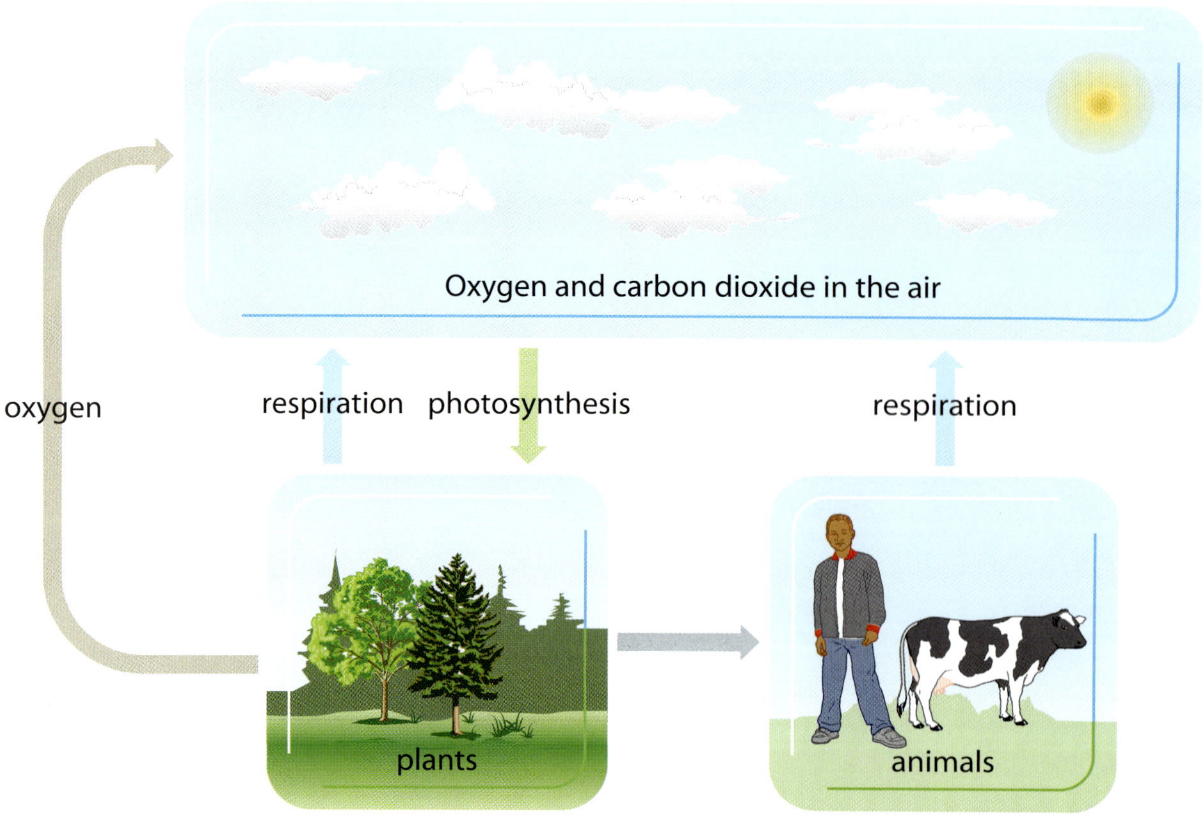

Every green plant has flowers. Some flowers are bright colours. Some are green, like the rest of the plant.

Flowers are high up on the stems. Some are blown about by the wind. Brightly coloured flowers attract insects. All flowers of every colour produce seeds.

The male part of a flower is the stamen. This is made of **anthers** which are on long stalks called filaments. The anthers produce pollen.

Some anthers hang outside the flower in the wind. Some stamens stand up. Insects that visit the flower brush past the stamens.

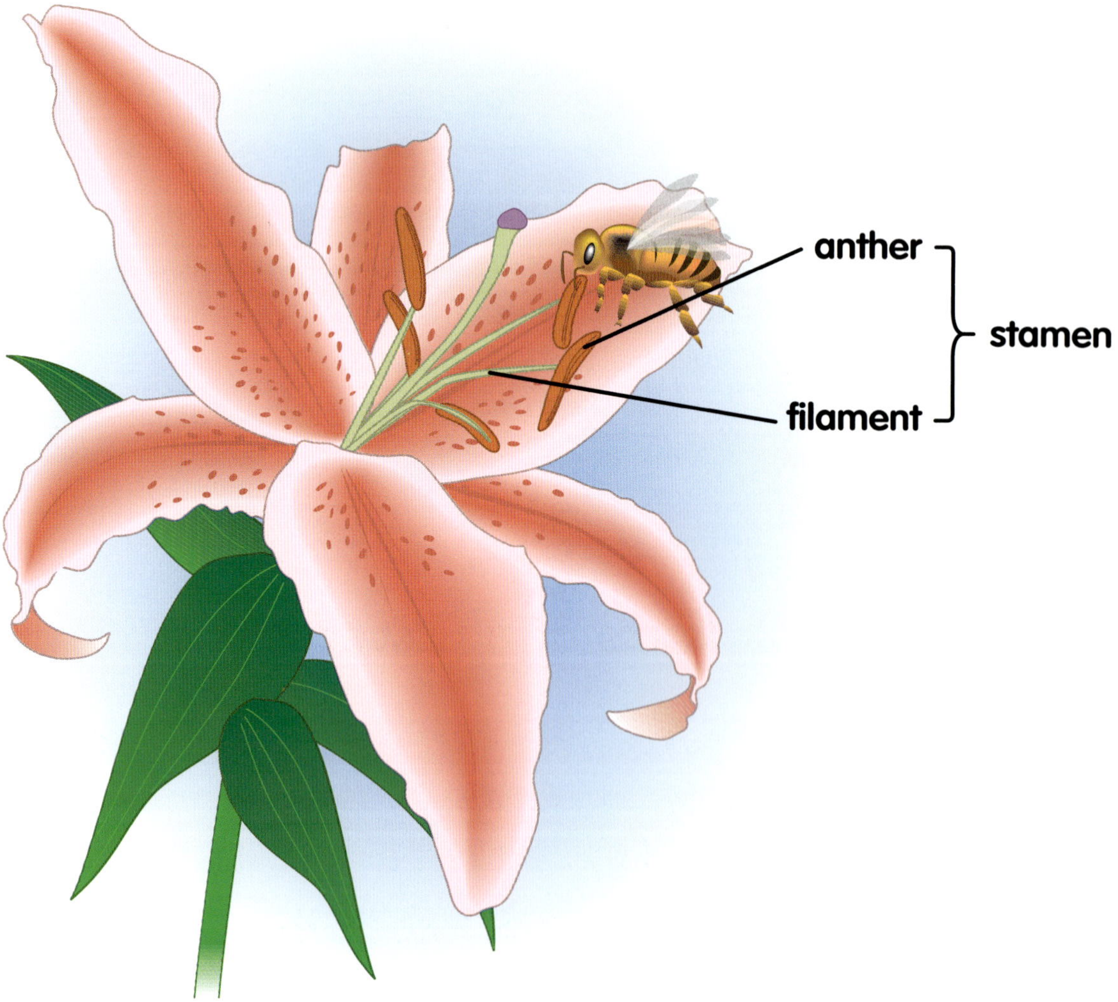

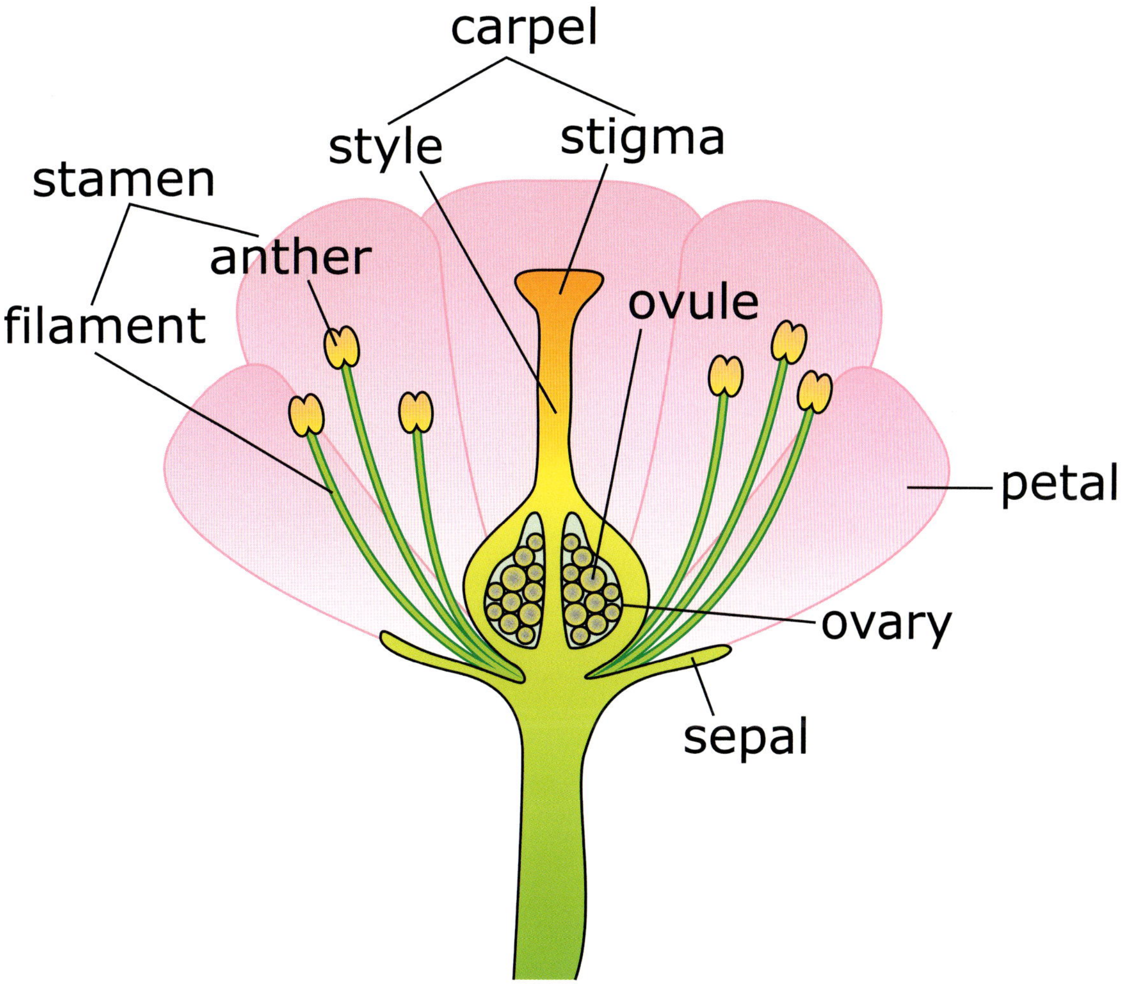

Parts of a flower

The carpel is the female part of a flower. Inside is the egg cell or ovum. The ovum is made by the ovule. Above the ovule is a style, and at the tip of the style is the stigma.

The style holds the stigma up. Insects that visit the flower brush past the stigma.

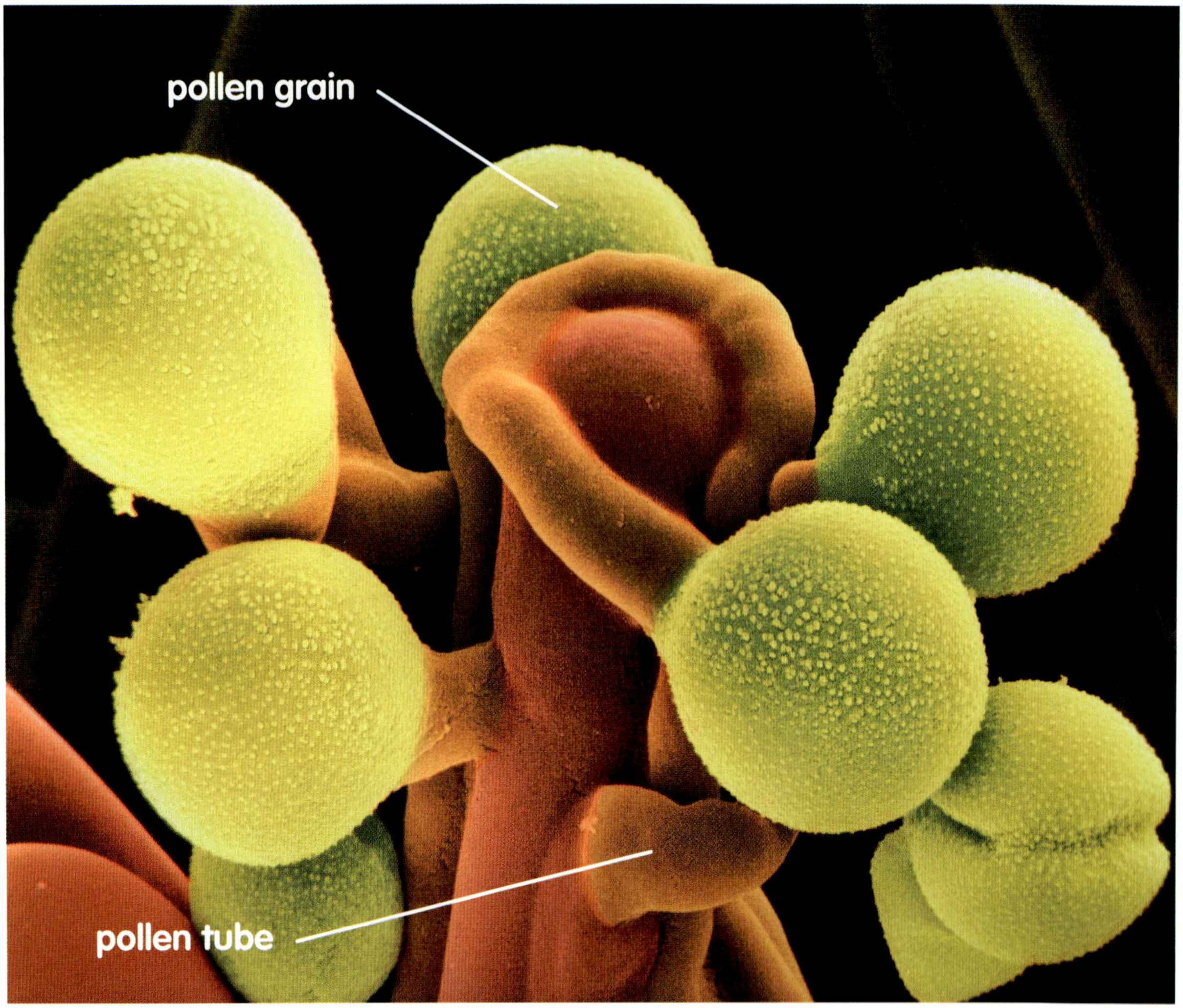

Magnified photograph

Pollen is made of grains as fine as dust. A seed is produced when a pollen grain is carried to a stigma. The male pollen **fertilises** the female egg cell or ovum.

The ovum is in the ovule. The ovule will not grow into a seed without the pollen.

A pollen grain from the male part of one flower lands on the stigma of another. A tube grows from the pollen grain down through the style. A cell from the pollen grain fertilises the ovule.

A fertilised seed begins to grow.

Magnified photograph of pollen grains on a stigma

Pollen travels from flower to flower. Some pollen is carried on the wind. The anthers of these flowers are long, hanging in the wind. The stigma is long, too.

Plants **pollinated** by the wind don't need bright flowers. They can be green, like the rest of the plant. Grass flowers are green.

Insects and other animals carry pollen from flower to flower. Flowers make a sweet liquid called nectar. Insects visit flowers for the nectar. Pollen brushes on the insect's coat. It goes to another flower, and the stigma brushes the pollen off.

Flowers that are pollinated by insects are brightly coloured and smell strongly. The colours and smell attract insects.

The fertilised ovule begins to grow into a seed. The fertilised egg cell is inside. Around it is a food store and a seed coat.

In many plants, the seeds are contained in a fruit. The fruit protects the seed and helps disperse it. For example, coconut fruits protect the seed inside.

If new plants grew next to the parent plant, the plants would be crowded. They would compete for the same sunlight and water. So seeds are **dispersed**. They are spread around.

Some are blown by the wind. They may be very light. They may have **wings** or a parachute.

Some seeds are dispersed by animals. They may be carried on the outside of the animal. These seeds have hooks and spikes to catch on the animal's fur.

Some seeds are carried inside the animal. The animal eats the fruit for food. The seeds pass out of the animal with its waste. The seeds are carried far from the parent plant.

Some seeds are dispersed by water. They fall into a river or the sea. The seeds float on the water. They are carried far from the parent plant.

Some seeds are fired from the plant. Part of the plant twists or bursts. The seeds fall far from the plant. They are dispersed.

Many seeds do not grow into new plants. They may be eaten by animals. They may be eaten by humans. Rice is a seed, and bread is made from seeds of wheat plants ground into flour.

Some seeds find a place to grow. Then they germinate. First a root, and then a shoot, grow from the seed. The shoot pushes up through the ground. The roots grow down and **anchor** the plant. It becomes a seedling. The seedling grows into a new plant.

Some seeds have seed leaves inside them. The seedling carries the seed leaves up to the surface. They turn from white to green and become the plant's first leaves.

Some seedlings have no seed leaves. The shoot grows new, true leaves. The new leaves are green and the plant begins to make its own food.

The story from seed to seed is called a life cycle. A cycle is something that goes round. A plant's life cycle goes round.

This is a plant life cycle:

What if the life cycle is broken? If the flower is not pollinated, no seeds will grow. If there are seeds but nowhere suited to them, the seeds will not germinate. There will be no seedlings. The life cycle must be complete for new plants to grow.

Honeybees pollinate many food plants. Many honeybees are dying. Without honeybees, the flowers would not be pollinated. There would be no seeds or fruits. Without seeds, there will be no new plants, either.

Activities

Find out about honeybees where you live.

Test your friends

In pairs/small teams, choose 10 to 15 new or difficult words about life cycles. Write down and learn their English definitions.

Read out a definition. Ask the other person/team for the word it defines. If they cannot guess the word, you win a point. If they guess correctly, they win a point. Continue until you have used all your words. Make it more fun by asking the other person/team to spell the answer too. If they spell it correctly, they get an extra point.

Try this as a writing quiz too. Write only the definitions on paper. Exchange lists with the other person/team. Then write down the answers. This time, you only score a point if you spell the word correctly.

Glossary

anchor: to secure firmly in position

anther: the part of the male flower that contains pollen

carbon dioxide: a gas in the air that is a waste product of life, used by plants to help make food; the gas that people produce when breathing out

dispersal: the process that spreads seeds around so that they live far away from the parent plants

fertilise: a seed is fertilised when a cell from male pollen combines with a cell from a female ovum

germination: a seed germinates when it starts to grow into a new plant

oxygen: a gas in the air that is essential for most life; used by plants and animals to help break down food

pollination: when pollen is carried to the stigma of a plant

wings: part of a bird's or insect's body that it uses to fly